TRUE STORIES OF
Animal Antics

BY ARNOLD RINGSTAD

Published by The Child's World®
1980 Lookout Drive • Mankato, MN 56003-1705
800-599-READ • www.childsworld.com

Acknowledgments
The Child's World®: Mary Berendes, Publishing Director
Red Line Editorial: Editorial direction
The Design Lab: Design
Amnet: Production

Photographs ©: QiuJu Song/Shutterstock Images, cover (left),
back cover (top left), 1 (left), 2–3, 10, 12, 22; Eric Isselee/
Shutterstock Images, cover (top), 21; Rex Features/DZG/AP
Images, cover (center), 1 (center), 9; BrandX Images, cover
(bottom right), 1 (top right), 1 (bottom right), 3 (top right), 3
(bottom right), 8, 18; Anan Kaewkhammul/Shutterstock Images,
back cover (top right), 15; Mark Sisson/Rex Features/AP
Images, back cover (bottom), 6, 7; Shutterstock Images, 4; Rex
Features/AP Images, 5; Alexandr Dobysh/AP Images, 10; Eliza
Wiley /The Independent Record/AP Images, 11; Geoff Moore/
Rex Features/AP Images, 13; Ricardo De Mattos/Thinkstock,
14–15; Stephen Repasky/AP Images, 17; Dan Callister/Rex
Features/AP Images, 19; Alachua County Sheriff's Office/AP
Images, 20

ISBN 9781626873568
LCCN 2014930695

Printed in the United States of America
Mankato, MN
July, 2014
PA02225

ABOUT THE AUTHOR

Arnold Ringstad lives in Minnesota. His cat gets up to all kinds of silly antics.

CONTENTS

ANIMAL ANTICS

Animals sometimes act in surprising ways. Silly animals can be funny to watch. Dancing bears and lemur thieves are just two examples of animals acting strangely. Want to learn more about these and other animal antics? Keep reading!

Lemurs get up to all sorts of animal antics.

Horses in the House

Most horses live in barns or fields. They **gallop** around and eat hay. But Lucien and Amigo are not like most horses. They live on a farm with their owner, Sharon Taylor. The farm is in Ayrshire, Scotland. These horses don't stay inside a barn. They come in the house whenever they want!

Lucien and Amigo play with the family cat and dog. Taylor says they also try to help bring groceries into the house. The horses do get in the way sometimes. Taylor says they often stand at the dinner table. They help themselves to food. Still, she knows her horses are special. She said, "They aren't like normal horses. People do think it is strange, especially when they see our cat Samson getting a lift on their backs." There's one thing the horses have not figured out yet. They can't go up stairs. But Taylor thinks they may figure out how to climb them someday.

Amigo likes to keep his owners company in their kitchen.

The Dancing Bear

Brown bears live across northern Europe, Asia, and North America. Adult brown bears can weigh more than 1,000 pounds (450 kg). People think of bears as dangerous creatures. It's true that full-grown bears are big and strong. They can defend themselves fiercely. But brown bears do not always act **aggressively**.

British nature photographer Mark Sisson saw something strange in 2013. He was watching a family of brown bears in Finland. A mother bear was eating with her cubs.

Suddenly, one of the cubs stood up on its back legs. It started to move in a way that looked like dancing! Sisson started taking pictures. The cub swayed from side to side. It raised its front legs in the air. At first, the cub seemed shy about dancing. But then it danced again in front of its family.

However, its family was not impressed. Sisson said, "Unfortunately all he got was a disapproving look from [mom] and the rest of the family carried on eating!"

This bear cub gave his family a funny show.

A Lemur Thief

Lemurs are small mammals that look like monkeys. They have large eyes and striped tails. Lemurs come from the island of Madagascar in Africa. Many live in zoos around the world. But most aren't as silly as one at Dudley Zoological Gardens.

About 30 lemurs live at this English zoo. Usually, they live and play in the trees. But one rainy day, a lemur named Leon stayed on the ground. A zoo guest with an umbrella walked near Leon. The lemur saw this as his chance to stay dry.

Leon ran up to the guest. He grabbed the umbrella. Then, he walked around his one-acre (4,000 sq m) living space. Leon held the umbrella above his head to stay dry. However, a **gust** of wind came through. It almost blew him over! After that, Leon dropped the umbrella. He looked for another way to stay dry.

FUN FACT

Lemurs have soft, wide fingers. Their fingers help them clean other lemurs' fur. It also helps them grip umbrellas!

Leon carrying the umbrella.

The Money-Eating Dog

Sometimes, pets cause trouble. A cat may scratch furniture. A dog might chew up sneakers. But a dog named Sundance took trouble to a whole new level.

Sundance belongs to Wayne Klinkel. They live in Helena, Montana. Sundance had eaten things made of paper in the past. Still, Klinkel didn't think he needed to worry. He left Sundance alone in a car for a few minutes. He also left five $100 bills in the car.

When Klinkel came back, the money was missing. Just a small scrap of one bill was left. He figured out what had happened. Sundance had eaten the money! Klinkel followed Sundance around for the next few days. He collected the dog's waste. He later went through it. He found tiny scraps of money.

Klinkel cleaned the scraps. He taped them back together into bills. He sent

Sundance ate five $100 bills such as these.

them to the U.S. Treasury. That is the part of the government that prints money. Almost one year later, he got something in the mail from the treasury. It was a check for the $500 Sundance had eaten!

Sundance, who only has one eye, holds the check from the U.S. Treasury.

A Playful Octopus

Octopuses are sea creatures with eight legs. They use **gills** to breathe. They breathe in by sucking water into their gills. They breathe the water out through a hole called a funnel. One octopus in England breathes in a way that's fun for visitors to experience.

The octopus lives at Weymouth Sea Life Park in Dorset. Workers noticed he was a curious animal. The octopus poked his head over the top of his tank to look around. A worker

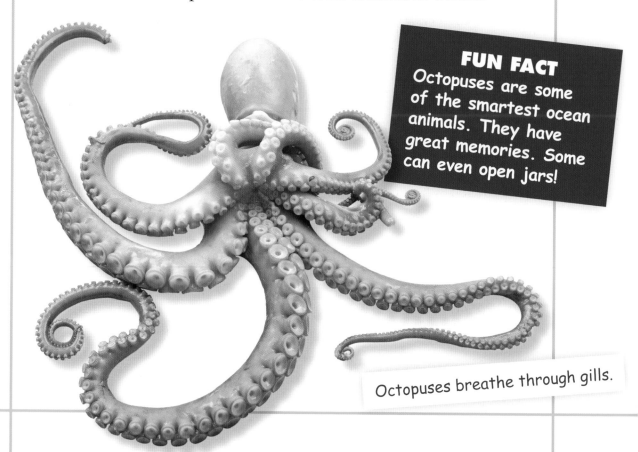

FUN FACT
Octopuses are some of the smartest ocean animals. They have great memories. Some can even open jars!

Octopuses breathe through gills.

Squirt takes aim at a man at Weymouth Sea Life Park.

explained what happened next. He said, "Then he realized that if he breathed out while he was doing that he could fire a stream of water like a hose."

That is how the octopus got his nickname. People started calling him Squirt. Workers clean his tank every other day. Every time, Squirt sprays them with water. Scientists aren't sure why Squirt does this.

The Gliding Eagle

Sea eagles live all around the world. One kind of sea eagle is the bald eagle. It is the national bird of the United States. Other kinds of sea eagles live in Australia. One eagle was seen doing something unusual in 2012. It happened in Sydney, Australia.

It was Katrina Lee's birthday. Her husband Richard bought her a **hang gliding** lesson. She soared through the sky with a group of other people. Richard got out his camera to

take pictures. But he noticed something strange. A sea eagle was following the hang gliders!

The eagle flew with the gliders for a few minutes. Then, it landed on one of them! It sat on the glider for about ten seconds before taking off. Soon, it came back and landed on a different hang glider.

Instructors had seen eagles flying with hang gliders before. But they had never seen an eagle take a ride on one!

Sea eagles sometimes fly with hang gliders.

Bees at the Airport

Honeybees are insects that live in **hives**. Queens lead the hives. Most of the bees in a hive are the queen's children. Sometimes, the old hive fills up or the old queen dies. Either way, the bees need to find a new place to live. In 2013, a group of bees picked a strange place for a new hive. They headed for a Pittsburgh, Pennsylvania, airport.

Passengers for a flight to New York were waiting to board their plane. Workers were getting ready to refuel the plane. Suddenly, they noticed a huge number of bees on the plane! A swarm of about 10,000 honeybees covered part of the wing. And they weren't going anywhere.

Airport workers had to call a professional beekeeper. He was able to remove the insects safely. He moved them away from the airport.

FUN FACT
Honeybee queens lay an amazing number of eggs. One queen can lay up to 1,500 eggs a day!

Honeybees made their home on an airplane's wing.

Nesting in a Traffic Light

House sparrows live all across North America. As their name suggests, they live near people's houses. The birds build nests in nooks and crannies. Some live in big buildings in cities. Others live in barns in the country. One family of sparrows made an unusual home in New York City. They built their nest inside a traffic light!

Photographer Dan Callister noticed the sparrows in April 2012. They were inside the yellow light of a traffic signal. Callister took photos of the nest. But when he returned the next day, the nest was gone! A newspaper checked with the Department of Transportation. But it said it had not removed the nest. What happened to the sparrows' nest was a mystery.

However, the sparrows didn't give up. The day after, they returned. The birds started building a new nest in the same spot.

Look for bird nests in traffic lights.

House sparrows in New York City make a nest in a traffic light.

Chomping on a Police Car

This alligator took his anger out on a police car.

More than 1 million alligators live in Florida. Usually, they stay in rivers or swamps. But sometimes they meet people. Their bites can be deadly. When alligators show up in places humans live, people often call the police.

In May 2011, someone spotted a seven-foot (2.1 m) alligator near a golf course. The police showed up and parked their car near it. They called an alligator trapper and waited for him to arrive. While they were waiting, the alligator became aggressive. The gator walked over to the police car and bit its front bumper!

The gator refused to let go of the bumper. One officer got into the car. He slowly backed it up. Finally, the alligator let go. The police later said that the gator's powerful bite had badly damaged the car.

Alligators can become aggressive.

aggressively (uh-GRES-iv-lee) When something acts aggressively, it is ready to fight. Brown bears sometimes act aggressively.

currency (KUR-en-see) Currency is money. The U.S. Treasury collects damaged currency.

gallop (GAL-up) To gallop is to run. Horses gallop in fields.

gills (gilz) Gills are body parts that fish and other water animals use to breathe. Octopuses breathe through their gills.

gust (gust) A gust is a sudden, strong wind. A gust of wind almost took Leon the lemur's umbrella away.

hang gliding (hayng GLYED-ing) Hang gliding is using a large wing and harness to glide through the air. An eagle flew with people as they went hang gliding.

hives (hyevz) Hives are where bees live. Bees build hives in strange places, such as airports.

BOOKS

125 True Stories of Amazing Animals: Inspiring Tales of Animal Friendship and Four-Legged Heroes, Plus Crazy Animal Antics. Washington, DC: National Geographic, 2012.

125 True Stories of Amazing Pets: Inspiring Tales of Animal Friendship and Four-Legged Heroes, Plus Crazy Animal Antics. Washington, DC: National Geographic, 2014.

Gould, Francesca. *Why Dogs Eat Poop: Gross But True Things You Never Knew About Animals.* New York: G.P. Putnam's Sons, 2013.

Newman, Aline Alexander. *Ape Escapes! And More True Stories of Animals Behaving Badly.* Washington, DC: National Geographic, 2012.

WEB SITES

Visit our Web site for links about animal antics:
childsworld.com/links

Note to Parents, Teachers, and Librarians:
We routinely verify our Web links to make sure they are safe and active sites. So encourage your readers to check them out!